HERE

HERE

A Happy Book
About Existence

Dr. Sharenda Roam

Dedication

To Isabeau, my darling daughter.

I love you forever and always!
There is beauty and joy HERE.

Live while you live, my love!

Acknowledgments

Thank you to my dad and mom
for teaching me
how to live while you live!

Contents

Prologue

You are HERE. You made it. From the Mystery, from the seemingly random, purposeful kiss of an egg and sperm, you arrived. You are on planet Earth. Welcome, amazing Earthling!

This book is about the spiritual, intellectual, and physical juiciness of life we Earthlings get to experience. Sure, if there's life on Saturn, they get to experience all those colorful rings. But here we have music, laughter, flowers, babies, giraffes, chocolate, and so much more. These writings are for those of us already here and those who will be arriving on this beautiful green-and-blue planet, floating in space.

HERE is a book for my children and my grandchildren and for any child of God who needs to hear these words. And if you were wondering . . . yes . . . I do believe the children are our future. Thank goodness, because I think most of us are pretty tired at the end of our lives, especially if we live till gravity makes the skin of our earlobes and elbows long and jiggly.

This book is a conversation between you and me. Sometimes I will speak in the first person, sometimes directly to you, and in other stanzas I will be hugging you with my words. Make a cup o' tea, light a candle, turn on your music, and let's chat.

I'm glad you're HERE!

I

Oh, Mystery

How did we get here, all of us, on this floating green-and-blue planet in space? In the beginning, God. What is the beginning? How did we become aware that we are conscious?

When God spoke the world into existence, I wonder what God's voice sounded like? Like a triumphant roar that shook mighty mysteries to create matter and energy? Like a woman in labor birthing a miracle and bringing life from the unseen to the seen, manifesting a fleshly visible form from the invisible? From chaos and order, logic and wildness, darkness and colors, light and water, pain and blood, flesh and joy, we *became*. I would have loved to have been there, watching and experiencing every moment. Maybe we were there and have forgotten how the Creative One breathed life into zebras, butterflies, buffalos, trees, rivers, seaweed—and you and me.

Can you imagine how it must have felt to hear the first whale sing as it experienced the weightlessness of its massive body swimming through a salty sea? To see a tiny, newly created bird spread its wings and lift in flight, chirping with the joy of coming to life? To watch the first horse gallop and whinny, with its mane and tail flying in the wind? To see a man watch a woman as she takes her first breath and opens her eyes, declaring to love him forever?

Oh, Mystery, thank you, for everything.

All Is New

There are no two things exactly alike on our planet. We find uniqueness in every drop of rain, each snowflake, every animal, and within each human. There may be four leaves on a clover, but each leaf will be special and different. Every tiny piece of soil has its own shape.

Each cloud that rolls across the sky flows with its own rhythm. Every time we laugh, cry, dance, and sing, we move in a neoteric way. Some say there is nothing new under the sun, but there is newness in every single day. Even down to the microscopic, each atom is distinct in the way it pulses and vibrates.

We are continually being renewed in every cell.

Awaken to the eternal newness of life!

All is new, including me and you.

3

String Theory

Let's go to the molecular level, down to the nitty-gritty dirt band. Music, according to the string theory, vibrates within our lives. String theory proclaims that in the deepest recesses of our beings, inside our atoms, in our deepest quarks (not quirks), are dancing, vibrating strings. In other words, you and I are musical instruments from the inside out. This is why when we hear a groove, we tap our feet, clap our hands, and shake our bootays! We can't help it! It's how we are constructed. You may not be dancing on the outside for everyone to see, but you, my dear reader, are dancing on the inside! Let it out! Let it go! Now, why do some scientists believe this theory when they can't see the strings with our current technology? Albert Einstein looked for a unified field theory that would be the grand underlying principle that gives us the recipe, the formula for all of existence. Some scientists believe the string theory may be just this. In fact, sometimes the string theory is described as possibly being the "theory of everything" (TOE). I really like this theory, and yet I wonder, *What is inside the string? What is inside the toe?* My toenails are painted bubble-gum pink right now. I feel like dancing. Join me. Get up on your feet and dance!

Music is magical. It is the beating in your chest and the joy in your hips! Enjoy it as much and as often as possible while you are here!

4

Vegetable Garden

I planted a vegetable garden in my backyard. One Husky Cherry Tomato plant, one Giant Tomato plant, and two Early Girl Tomato plants line the back of my raised bed. Standing in front are squash, cucumber, pepper, and cantaloupe plants. I learned from my cousin that we used to have thousands of varieties of vegetables, and now we only have hundreds. The ones called "heirloom" are originals and have not been made into hybrid vegetables. Heirloom Vegetables—they sound ancient, strong, and delicious. I hope to plant more vegetables and never have to go to the grocery store again except for chocolate, unless I start growing cacao beans and sugar cane and get a milk cow, then I could make chocolate. Oh, I also need salt. I can get that from the ocean.

I have an orange tree in my backyard too. Have you ever smelled orange blossoms? Those little white flowers smell like fresh sweetness; it's probably what Heaven smells like, truly an olfactory delight.

5

Plant Something

Self-sustainability is a worthy endeavor. Most of us pay someone else for everything we need to survive: shelter, food, water, and then of course luxuries as well: clothes, shoes, electricity, tools, entertainment, knowledge/education, medical treatments, spa treatments, etc. What if I grew all my own fruits and vegetables (or traded with neighbors), had a milk cow and some hens for laying eggs (or traded with neighbors), squatted on some land and built a house there from . . . um, the trees (I could get the tools and nails from a blacksmith neighbor), and sewed my own clothes (from the wool of my lamb)? Well, okay . . . I guess we could keep going. I think we already lived this way in the Middle Ages, and I think some people still practice this lifestyle. It sounds like a lot of hard work, but kind of fun, in a village sort of way. Anyhoo, back to the twenty-first century in the city.

Plant something. It will ground you and help you grow.

Water

We need it! We crave it! It is necessary for life. It is part of us. The ultimate destination of water is the sea, until it vaporizes and rises to the sky, until it condenses and falls to the Earth where the cycle continues. It flows, it hardens, it cleanses, it carves paths in stone, it gives life, it forms bonds, it separates. It is tenacious and does what it will. It is flexible and changes form. It is, like many natural processes (wind, sun, gravity), out of human control. We dam it and it finds a crack. We cook with it and it becomes steam. It fills our bodies and releases in the form of our tears (liquid emotion that seeps out when we experience extreme joy or sadness). We freeze it and it melts in our drinks. We break its surface and swim in its embrace. What a wonderful, dynamic creation! Water! Words cannot fully describe this element.

We can become like water, flowing around obstacles, passive and serene, yet full of power that can carve a grand canyon. Waterfalls and mountain streams flow to their ultimate destination: the ocean. We find spiritual strength in living water, water that fills our spirits with tenacity and strength, wisdom and power. Become like it—passive and powerful! I'm thirsty for some H_2O!

Drink it often. Swim in it as much as possible. Soak in this magical elixir. Your body is a salty ocean. Is this why we are drawn to the beach? Grab your board and go surfing.

7

Sex

Speaking of things that are wet and salty . . .

You know what? This is a topic that requires some deep evaluation. And I need to talk about it right now because it is on my mind and I can't concentrate on anything else. I won't go into any more details, but right now my physiologic system is overriding my neurologic system, and all I can think about is this topic. It seems so natural yet complex. It is natural. All animals that I can think of do some form of this. But it gets complex even with them: mating dances, fighting, clashing antlers, butting heads, taking control over the pack. You know what I am talking about—sex! It deserves that exclamation point! We have all kinds of books discussing sex. We have sex therapists, sex addicts, sexually transmitted diseases, and more. It really has gotten complex. Some people practice polygyny (one man, multiple wives), and a few practice polyandry (one woman, multiple husbands). However, it seems that today, monogamy tends to be the preferred route in a committed relationship. Perhaps the beauty of it is in its complexity. If it was too simple, we wouldn't be as interested in it, not as many babies would be born, and the human race might become extinct. All I know is sex is beautifully complex, deliciously tart, emotionally packed, and passionate and peaceful all at the same time. It heightens all of our senses—taste, touch, smell, sight, sound—and takes us, with that sweet pattern of repetition, to another land. It has dark sides—bitterness, jealousy, pain—

but oh, it is all worth the color, joy, depth, juice, and beloved wildness. All in all, it comes down to how you use sex. Your body gains the rewards and suffers the consequences of how you use it, abuse it, pamper it, cherish it. Most people will admit that when you have sex, something magical happens. Thankfully, we choose who we share that magic with; who we allow into our sacred temple: a complete stranger, an abusive person, a kind person, the love of our life, or all of the above. And watch out for the consequences! They can be devastating or delightful, depending on our choices. An older wise woman once told me, "Just remember when you have sex, you are also having it with every person he had sex with." Okay, that's pretty gross but kind of true. Sex. It is as hot as a forest fire, wet as a hurricane, delicious as _____ (your favorite food/drink), and spiritually sacred. S.E.X.

Marry your love and treat your body like the sacred temple that it is.

8

Relationships

A relationship is like a garden. You have to water it, feed it, prune it, and give it lots of fresh air and sunshine. A little water is good; too much water and we can drown it. Feeding it—well, at this point I think I'll quote my great-grandma on her marriage advice, which has been passed down in my family for years. Her advice for a new bride to keep her husband happy was, "Keep his belly full and his balls empty." My great-grandmother was a little naughty. I'm not offering that advice; that was my great-grandma's thought. She was Shawnee, adopted into the Cherokee tribe, and had her own farm in Oklahoma given to her by the US government. A traveling preacher stopped by their home and, as a result of his influence, she became a Pentecostal. I only met her once, but her legend is alive in my family. And her marital words of encouragement have helped our family grow for generations to come.

When it comes to pruning your relationship, you have to watch out for suckers. Suckers are sprouts that grow on trees; they suck out the nutrients but produce no fruit. By doing this they steal the nutrients the tree needs for growing fruit. I have cut these off our grapefruit and lemon trees. Suckers can come in a variety of forms in a relationship. Just like with plants, you need to nip them in the bud. Suckers might show up in the form of other humans or even emotions, like jealousy or insecurity.

Some great advice I once received was: "You either break your expectations or you break your relationship." This is especially true in marriage. Most of us go into relationships with expectations. Healthy expectations are those that anticipate love and kindness from the other person. But expectations that include the man being a very wealthy prince of a small country who invites his girl to live in a castle with manicured gardens full of colorful wild birds and wandering deer might be a bit much. But in general, if you go into a relationship with expectations that are not met, you may break that relationship, then go into another one with those same expectations and break that one; thus, the destructive cycle continues. I am not saying it is easy. Marriage is definitely its own school, one with no final graduation ceremony. But enough of that, let's return to romance.

I now have a golden band on my left hand and am relishing being married to the prince of my heart. Oh, let me tell you a bit of our story. Skip this part if you do not want to feel rapturously joyful and full of romance. Or fix a cup of chamomile tea and indulge yourself in the merriment.

So there we were . . .

Him, with his eyes the color of a stormy sea, curly locks of hair, tanned skin, and a soul full of deep Earth wisdom, waiting . . . for me. The music began playing "Dance of the Sugar Plum Fairy," my cue to begin walking toward the love of my life, my destiny, my honey-babe. With my curls up in a creative do that included clouds of white tulle that wound in and out of my hair extensions, held in place with hundreds of bobby pins, hairspray, and a stunning sparkly gold flower clip, my wedding dress and

I glided down the aisle. I daresay we floated. This was partly due to my feeling of ecstasy from the countless pain pills I had taken that morning to stop the throbbing of my newly cracked-to-the-root tooth. I would not let that stop me from enjoying my castle garden wedding with my bridesmaids, who wore petal-pink gowns surrounded by décor of moss, lanterns, candles, and fresh bouquets. If you want to see pictures, you can go to my Pinterest page and look for my board called "Wedding." At this point, over 8000 of my Pinterest friends have decided they, too, like my wedding vibe. Oh, joy!

Okay, how did we arrive at this perfect day? Well, let's go back in time. Yes, we met (although I knew Jeff when we were younger), got engaged in nine days, and married six months later. I had a boyfriend at the time; a nice enough chap but one who was going a different direction than me in life. My mom, sister, and cousin all decided I should take notice of Jeff. Jeff would be in town July fourth weekend, and perhaps we could hang out and get to know one another better. Well, we definitely connected. Three days later he asked me to be his girl. I told him I needed to make a phone call to my boyfriend. And here we are, married and crazy—so crazy in love.

He is forest magical. I told him so, and added, "You look like you could be the king of the wood nymphs." To which he did not reply; he only gave me a quizzical look.

I hope you find your own prince or princess of your heart.

9

Friendships

I love my friends! We must choose wisely when choosing friends. There are those who will celebrate us and those who will try to tear us down. Some will shorten our lives, and others will lengthen them. Show me your friends, and I will show you your future. Be choosy with whom you give your time. Our time here is limited, and none of us knows how many days we will be gifted.

But, oh, those scrumptious friendships! The ones that lift us higher, make us feel like we are flying after sharing dreams and inspirations over a cup of tea. These friendships are special delights. Kindred spirits, the ones we know we can be completely vulnerable with and they will listen, without judgment, and love us unconditionally. These friendships—they are rare and deep. We treasure them.

Sometimes these kindred friendships are for a season; sometimes they are for a lifetime. What a gift are lifetime friends! The memories we share are like lovebirds on the branches of our hearts.

True friends will inspire you to trust yourself, as they often confirm what you already know, but sometimes need to hear from a voice outside of yourself.

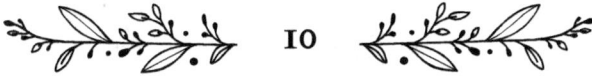

Shift

One of the greatest superpowers we have is the ability to shift our thinking. When an unwanted thought comes along, we can shift it down another path. Belief grows as we do this. When a sorrowful thought comes, we can shift it to a joyous one. When a fearful thought comes, we can shift it to a courageous one. We are conductors of our thoughts. Shift the track and don't look back. We create the destinations for our thoughts when we learn how to shift.

May I share an example with you? Thank you, dear reader.

During certain moments when grieving the loss of my mom, I shifted my thoughts from missing her to picturing her in a gorgeous place beyond our world and enjoying being reunited with my dad, who had gone before her. Every time I shifted my thoughts, I sent my emotions to a different destination.

When I choose to shift my thoughts, my whole body responds and follows my mind. Do this and you will experience the luxury of mental discipline.

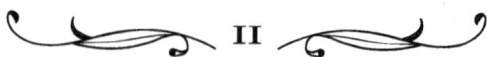

II

Compassion

Compassion can become dangerous when it becomes your romantic passion. Have you ever been in a relationship with someone you felt needed "fixing"? Being compassionate is a lovely trait to have, but when the person you feel compassion for becomes your romantic "project," it can become dangerous. How? The energy you put into that person can eventually drain you into exhaustion; even worse, it can drag you in and overtake you. As one of my wise friends told me, "Sharenda, if you keep playing with fire, eventually you will get burned." It might feel thrilling for now, but if you marry that person, be ready for a lifetime of suffering. We are not here to be saviors for those who don't want to open up their own gates of hell and let themselves out. Because guess what? When they open those gates and let us inside their personal hell, it can be hard to escape. Even if you don't plan to marry the person, the temporary waste of time can make it hard to breathe and will likely burn your heart. If I had it to do over again, I wouldn't waste my energy on these relationships. Does that sound too preachy? Good.

Be compassionate! But don't confuse your compassion with romantic passion!

Mother Teresa

It seems that one of the most compassionate people, Mother Teresa, also had to learn about compassion. I read that she gave away everything she had—her food, her clothes—in order to live like the people whom she was helping. Someone told her that if she continued this path, she could not help others. Instead of helping those in need, she would become one of the needy and then need help herself.

How did she learn to maintain strength even in serving the poorest of the poor? How can we equip ourselves with compassion in the same way to serve others?

A secret to Mother Teresa's great success in helping so many people is attributed to one of her prayers: *"The fruit of silence is prayer; the fruit of prayer is faith; the fruit of faith is love; the fruit of love is service; the fruit of service is peace."* She believed we are all children of God, and that we have been created to love and be loved.

When compassion, this divine gift that helps us overcome our own selfishness, prompts us to act, we must be prepared.

And preparation begins with sitting in silence.

13

Saints & Martyrs

In Christianity, saints are often martyrs. They are people who would not deny the truth, would not worship an emperor or earthly god, and/or whose faith would not be conquered by fearmongering.

We have this powerful instinct to deny ourselves when in a fight for ideas in which we believe, and it is unstoppable and vital in the right circumstances. However, when we don't temper this instinct in our earthly relationships with wisdom and boundaries, it can have devastating effects.

In fact, in our earthly relationships we must learn an important difference between being a saint and a martyr. A saint sacrifices, while a martyr is the sacrifice.

We have seen this in unhealthy relationships. One partner gives and sacrifices to the point of losing herself, even becoming an emotional bag lady, scraping for crumbs of love anywhere and everywhere. Until one day, by grace, she awakens with the realization that she is a loved child of God, made for greater things.

Mothers are great examples of self-sacrificing saints, but even mothers must learn not to be martyrs.

May we all learn the ways of saints and martyrs, in balance.

14

Practicing Perspective

Where do we seek wisdom? *Seek and you will find*, Scripture says. Is our perspective correct or an optical illusion? It is part of our human responsibility to get it right.

The world is a great teacher. Practicing perspective not only involves the brain, but also the soul. We can't always believe what we think. Assuming without correct knowledge is dangerous, as it can activate our emotions and our fight-or-flight instinct. Which, in turn, shapes our perspective. For example, if I assume a person is angry at me, when they are not, my perspective of him shifts. I may view him as temperamental, threatening, or weak. I develop a narrative about him that is incorrect. I may even tell others about him and treat him with malice or disdain. I am assuming something that is not the truth, thereby injuring a person through my thoughts and words.

Jesus said it this way,

> "You have heard that it was said to those of old, '*You shall not murder*,' and whoever murders will be in danger of the judgment. But I say to you that whoever is angry with his brother without a cause shall be in danger of the judgment." (Matthew 5:21–22 OSB)

When we gain a truthful perspective, our being comes into

alignment—mind, body, and soul—and we develop a love for others that is not possible without a correct perspective.

Our perspective is deeply influenced by our malleable brains. We determine our neural pathways by exercising our free will, evidenced in what we choose to read, watch, listen to, smell, touch, and allow into our innermost being.

The art of practicing perspective is developed through knowledge, discipline, and intention. You are magnificently created—precious, delicate, and mighty. What practices will you adopt in order to shape your perspective?

15

Body

Definition of *body*:

The sensitive, skin-covered, luscious clock of bones, drumming heart, pulsating veins, electric nerves, invisible reflexes, passionate hormones, and colorful, stormy consciousness. Your body is a masterpiece.

Imagine an abstract sculpture of your body. Would it be made of wood, copper, flowers? What colors would bring it to life?

How can you best honor your body?

You are made in the image of God.

You are a child of God.

Treat your body like you would your own child.

Darling, you are a gift to this world.

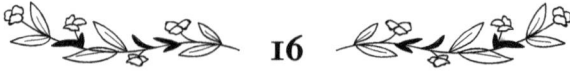

Engage

Our time here on Earth calls on us to engage. Let us pause and smell flowers, gaze at the stars, stand in awe of the consistent sun greeting us every morning. And the shining moon greeting us every night.

Let us lie in the tall grass, lick the dew off the stems, braid the strands, and smell the wet soil.

Let us touch the rough bark of a tree's skin and marvel at the shade and shelter it gives us.

Let us mimic a bird's song and reach out to communicate in their way instead of ours. Let us learn how they live, birth, and die.

Let us call on our elders, hug them, and treasure the wisdom they have to share. Let us remind them that they are loved and cherished.

Let us honor our children, no matter their age. Let us show them the joy of their existence and respect their fresh view of the world.

Let us feel jubilation in ourselves, in our own unique ways of being, doing, and dreaming. Let us show mercy to our thoughts and grace to our actions. And let us learn, stand back up, and begin again.

Let us love like we have never loved before.

Let us engage while we are here.

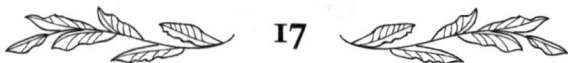

17

Wrinkles

I love my wrinkles.

I love them because they originated from squinting in the sun when I was thirteen years old on vacation with my family at the beach.

I love them because they remind me of when I laughed and laughed so hard, I cried (and peed a tiny bit).

Like sunbeams from the corners of my eyes, they travel across my skin.

I love them because I see them on the faces of my friends and my brother and my sister, reminding me we have traveled life together.

I love them because they make the same patterns on my face as on my mom's face.

I love them because they reveal that I have questioned and doubted and gained wisdom.

I love them because they tell my story.

On my honey-colored skin that holds my soul in tight, they create triangles and stars that shoot across my cheeks and streak from the corners of my eyes.

I love my wrinkles.

And I love yours too.

18

Do

Even the difficult times can be repurposed into a lesson. There are times when we feel sad and angry about an injustice. These emotions trigger when we hear something, see something, or read something about a particular issue. Instead of letting the injustice control your emotions, take charge of the injustice in your own way. It doesn't matter how large or small the injustice is; try to think of ways that you might help resolve the injustice. It can be as small as donating one dollar or as large as volunteering your time, or even changing one thing about your own lifestyle. Being kind to someone who is suffering from an injustice is impactful and eternal.

Don't become a victim of your thoughts and emotions. Take charge and help create a peaceful and just world. If we succumb to our feelings of overwhelm, we can contract analysis paralysis. Sometimes we need to take a break from analyzing and just do something—anything— toward transforming the issue. DO something. Do SOME thing. Do some THING.

19

Breath

God's breath of life fills every living thing on Earth. Trees exhale oxygen, and we inhale it. Every animal, plant, and being is alive with the breath of God. Breathe and remember we all share God's breath.

From the moment we take our first breath till the moment we take our last, we live and experience the blessings of being here. Our lungs expand, and oxygen from the eternal fills us. Breath came from the One who created oxygen, the One who created our lungs, the One who dreamed that within a vacuous universe there would be creatures who breathed.

And now we live and move and have our being in the same breath that our ancestors breathed. We breathe the exhaled oxygen of giant trees and tiny flowers; the last breath of dying saints and first breaths of newborn babies. In this way we are one; we are all children of the One.

Every breath is a gift. Inhale. Exhale. Smile. Breathe.

Meditate

Find a place in nature to sit and meditate. Perhaps it is under a tree, or in a garden. Try to find a spot away from human noise to hear the voices that God has given to birds, bees, and tiny creatures. The voices we rarely hear because they are so quiet. If you have exceptional hearing, you might even hear the sound of a piece of soil move as a blade of grass pushes its point out of the ground.

Perhaps you might even gain a better understanding of the Diné (referred to as Navajo) concept of Hózhó. This complex way of being in the world is a multidimensional intellectual construct that includes beauty, order, and harmony. We can gain a wealth of knowledge about creation, and ourselves, when we make the time.

Once you have found your sacred place, you might engage in a writing practice that will help you still your thoughts and focus on your immediate environment.

On a piece of paper write:

I see . . .

I hear . . .

I smell . . .

I taste . . .

I touch . . .

I feel . . .

I know . . .

Focus on the present moment. Engage your senses and write about what you are experiencing. Refresh. Renew. Revitalize. Energize your being.

Focus on being here.

Happiness

Happiness comes from knowing you are being the best person you can be. It comes from being honest with yourself. It thrives when you have positive, brand-new experiences. It comes from treating others well. Happiness deepens when you live up to your own expectations! Be yourself. Live well.

Choose happiness.

Thankfulness

One morning, I awoke in my little studio apartment with big windows in a neighborhood called Hillsboro Village and had a revelation, an aha moment. My unhealthy habit of waking up, unsure of how I would feel that day—sad or happy—needed to change. I was writing music and singing in Nashville's Music City scene, but that didn't mean I had to be a moody artist. Instead, I decided to create a new habit. Each morning, I would choose my first thought of the day. That thought would be, "I'm thankful." I am thankful for this day, for music, for life. I consciously selected this thought as my first for the next days, months, and years.

This little shift in thinking and this change of behavior altered my mood. Today, I still wake up with these thoughts. Thankfulness: this practice became a habit. I am thankful for dawn, twilight, and each star in the sky. I am thankful for you.

Choosing to be thankful will change your life and the lives of those around you for the better. Start each morning with a thankful thought.

23

Your Color

You are your own unique color in the painting kit of life, and what a vibrant and beautiful color you are! Look at your skin in the sunlight. It gleams with all the colors of the rainbow.

Your skin is like none other. It has its own hue and nuance. Only you get to wear this naturally lovely color. Sometimes I say out loud, "God, thank You for letting me be born as Sharenda."

My dear reader friend, you have exquisite skin!

If you could create a new color, what would it look like? What would you name it? Even our imagination, and the limits of our imagination, the colors that we can imagine are created by the Infinite Artist. I once asked a pastor if he thought there were colors we could not see. He answered that there may be colors we have never seen, but we are created with Earth eyes. In other words, our senses are uniquely tuned to the beauty here on Earth and in our Universe. I love this answer with its openness to possibilities and its truthful grounding pigment.

Your colors are perfect.

Hope

I once heard someone say that greatness is leaving a room and knowing that you left the people in the room with hope.

We all hope for things. Scientists hope for a breakthrough cure. Inventors hope for a successful, imaginative idea. Musicians hope for a hit song. Artists hope to paint a "Mona Lisa."

Hope is an emotion. It doesn't require proof or belief. One can doubt and still have hope. Hope is like love in the sense that you can feed it and it will grow. Unlike love, hope doesn't need an object of affection. It is something that a person can develop within herself. Sometimes hope requires courage. Hope is a spark that can spread throughout your being and burst into a fire of unspeakable joy.

Inside the word *hope* we find *hop*. Remember when you hopped as a kid? (btw: I love that baby goats are called kids.) We hopped for joy and the hope that life held.

Hope is an openness to possibilities.

Hope. It is the evidence of unseen delights.

Nature

You are nature. You are a fabulous mud ball full of life, consciousness, and wisdom. Like the trees, wave your branches. Like the birds, sing your songs. Like the wind, dance across this gorgeous green planet. You are part of her, and she is part of you. You need her. She is your sustenance. She nourishes you. Without Earth, where would we be? Literally? Where?

We are connected biologically, chemically, and atomically to nature. The plants clean our air with their exhalations. Have you ever wondered why you can breathe better in the forests and mountains where there are trees? Yep! Give credit to the amazing element called oxygen. We grow skin, and trees grow bark. If you are holding a book, you are touching a slice of tree, a slice of nature.

There are vast kingdoms of animals below our feet deep in the soil. Some of them are working hard to make new soil so we can grow fresh fruits and vegetables. The whole planet works together to sustain its living inhabitants. We are part of a vast web of life, an energy circle of living beings, walking, running,

and skipping across planet Earth, moving under her surface and swimming through her waters. Earth is a miraculous living ball, and we are part of her.

We are natural. We are nature.

I remember as a child making mud pies after it rained. I probably tried tasting one too. There's nothing like digging our fingers and toes in wet earth. At some level we know we are made of mud and magical matter, full of nutrients and the potential needed for life.

Today or next weekend, dig your bare toes in some mud. Don't worry about what anyone else thinks. They will be wishing they were doing it too.

Okay, mud ball, go do something nice for another mud ball! You're a miracle!

Communing

There is a deep longing in most humans to connect, to commune with the Divine. Anthropologists see evidence for this in the earliest humans on this planet. Archeologists have found small female figurines from the Paleolithic Era, or Old Stone Age. Some, but not all, of these have accentuated female elements, leading many scholars to believe these represent fertility. Thousands of these female figurines may be found throughout ancient history in a variety of cultures and areas around and within the Earth. Many scholars believe the earliest ideas about spirituality were related to the Earth and the weather. Therefore, Mother Earth was important as she brought forth food and sustenance, and the sky was important because it brought forth rain and sun.

The idea that there are forces at work leads us to seek to engage with these forces or the origin of these forces. Spirituality, then, is not something new; it is a part of us that is very, very old. Its forms and shapes are determined by the

cosmos (the sun, the moon, planets), the elements (earth, wind, water, fire), animals (sheep, goats, elephants, snakes), as well as a variety of other historic happenings, such as important human figures being born.

Although the way in which individuals choose to connect with the Divine may be different, the fact remains that there is a desire to commune. And sometimes this desire is not to ask for help or rain, but solely to feel a presence, a union with the Origin of everything.

Be still and know.

Commune with the Spirit.

Diversity

The diversity of life is like the sands of the sea. Multitudes of animals—microscopic, macroscopic, with stripes, spots, fur, feathers, scales, and skin—live together with us. Take a microscope and look at the life-forms in a drop of water. This vast array of diversity sustains life. If a gene pool becomes too small and lacks diversity, the species can go extinct. Imagine if all humans looked alike and thought alike. Imagine if all animals were pink giraffes. Life needs diversity to thrive.

What a brilliant concept, diversity in everything, a cure for boredom, and solution to extinction.

Rain

One of the most beautiful things we get to experience as Earthlings is rain. It is cleansing. It is life-giving. Water droplets from fluffy clouds high in the sky gift us with their outpouring. Sometimes it comes as a mist, other times with thunder and lightning. Its aroma is fresh as it turns our Earth green.

Let it rain!

Let it fall in our teapots.

Let's make tea.

And drink in the rain.

I Am

While sitting in the Denver airport waiting on a delayed flight, I decided to close my eyes and meditate. I began as I usually do, thinking in my mind, *Thank you, God.* I suddenly felt a strong urge to stop. It was like God was saying to me, "Stop talking to Me like I am somewhere out there and you are trying to reach Me. I am in you, and you are in Me. Rest. You are joy, and joy is you. You are peace, and peace is you."

Intentionally choose your identity. Let yourself be transformed into the image of Christ. There are seven *I am* statements in the book of John where Jesus stated, "I am . . ."

Let your *I am* reflect who you truly want to be.

30

It Just Works

I dreamed I was in a small cathedral, with its wooden benches and tall, beautiful stained-glass windows somewhere in London. The pastor was going to be gone and asked me if I would speak. As I thought about my topic, this idea came to me: "Following Jesus can make your dreams come true." And my tag line, the one the congregation would repeat throughout my sermon, was, "It just works." So, how does it work? "Do unto others as you would have them do unto you" just works. Almost every philosophical and ethical dilemma can be solved by placing it inside this thought.

At some point in our spiritual journey, we become so connected that our will can mesh with God's will. With this dynamic exchange, our deepest desires become linked with truth, and nothing else fulfills us like truth.

31

Loving Yourself

It feels strange to say this, but I will anyway. I am falling in love with the woman I am becoming. The woman I see stepping into the Payette River in a picture taken in Idaho. That woman is full of natural power, beauty, and confidence. She is whole, and she is full of class. She is creative and compassionate. She has surrendered yet remains tenacious. She's learning to communicate with animals and the trees, remembering her connection to the soil and waters. She is content to let people be their unique selves. Colors swirl around her, and love speaks through her lips. She is enraptured to be alive. Joy fills her being, and she walks in peace. Yes, it feels strange to write this, but it ultimately feels good—oh, so good.

May you feel the same someday about yourself, my dear reader.

Perhaps you already do.

32

Weather

Whether you love the weather or whether you don't, the weather is the Earth's way of maintaining herself and sustaining life.

After living in the hot desert of Phoenix, Arizona, for many years and complaining about the heat every summer, I finally decided to stop wishing the desert was something other than what she is. In order to grow my vegetable garden, she needs lots of water; I have to provide it because the sky does not. She is a desert. She gets minimal rain. I cannot ask her to be something different than what she is.

She has her own flora and fauna. We need the deserts and the rain forests, the mountains and the valleys. They each sustain unique forms of life.

Complaining about the weather is like arguing with a dog to be more like a bird.

The seasons are constant yet ever-changing. The cycles are the same, but the way they express themselves—with colorful leaves, sweet raindrops, snowflakes in unlimited designs, and new babies of all species—is effervescent.

Oh, the weather here in our troposphere! Vivacious!

Ripples

As I look at this enchanting glacial lake, with its tall pine trees and surrounding snow-capped Sawtooth Mountains, I watch the rhythm of its surface, the ripple effect. There are large ripples that become waves lapping against the shore and small ones that dance, one after another. Remarkably, the ripples appear orderly, with equal distances between them, pushing the surface of the water until their power diminishes. As I write this, two boats are passing by, and I can see the ripples beginning their journey toward the shore, toward me.

Like the boats cruising across the lake, our lives make ripples. Serene, glorious, impactful.

34

Drinking from a Flower

I watched as a hummingbird drank from a bright-pink hibiscus flower. She sipped the sweet nectar and swallowed it down her dainty neck. I drink from glasses, bottles, and cups. Oh, to drink from a flower!

35

I Imagine You

There you are, dear one, reading these words, breathing, knowing I am writing to you. You are amazing. What a lovely person inside and out you are: full of emotions, imagination, and a heart that beats its own rhythm. Look at the palm of your hand. It's completely unique. Touch your cheek. Say, "I love you." Tell yourself again: "I love you (your name)." It is a beautiful thing to truly love yourself. For this love fills your being like a rushing river overflowing to flood the lives of others.

Live While You Live!

A life well lived is a discipline and an art. When we are young, we are curious explorers, learning through experiences. As we gain understanding, we can put that knowledge to work, celebrating life through loving and serving others, making choices that serve and bring happiness to those around us. "LIVE WHILE YOU LIVE!" is the epitaph on my father's gravestone. Oh, how we miss the ones who loved us. He lived by this slogan, and what a life he lived—loving all, travelling around the world, celebrating each moment, and riding the winds of God's breath. He was rare, here and gone, leaving an example of a life well-lived.

Thank you, Dad, for modeling what an amazing man is. I promise to follow your quote and encourage others with this dynamic principle. LIVE WHILE YOU LIVE!

37

Precious & Bella

My two darling Shih Tzus, Precious and Bella, warm my heart. They are my fur babies. I don't care what anyone says, they are angels with wagging tails. Have you ever had a sweet, furry companion? If so, you know. All they expect from us are belly rubs and walks. All creatures great and small are our mysterious, miraculous Earth companions. My Shawnee people call them "relatives" in the sense that we are all a huge family of created beings here on the Earth. We express our divinity in how we treat them. Thank you, Creator, for sharing the joyous extravagance and diversity of your creativity.

38

Wealthy

There are different kinds of wealth. We can be wealthy in relationships, which is the best kind of wealth. But if you want to become wealthy with money, I recommend three things: education, creativity, and work.

Education: Do your best to gain all of the knowledge you can. Go to school! Go to school! Go to school! Earn the highest degree of education available to you. This helps you learn how society and the global community think. It's like giving you backstage passes to the world stage. Education is not just a means to a job; it provides a deeper understanding of the inner workings of humankind.

Creativity: Develop your imagination and learn (or open up to) creative skills. We are brilliantly creative beings. Find your favorite ways of creating – playing music, drawing, knitting, singing, sculpting, etc. – and make time for these. Creativity leads to innovation and fresh ways of doing life.

Work: I call it "crankin!" "Crank it out!" Do what you need to do to make it happen! When you know what needs to be done, take that first step (sometimes this is the hardest part), and the ball will roll. One way to work smarter so that you don't burn out is making work fun. For example, I love to teach, but I don't always enjoy grading exams and papers. Therefore, I create an environment that makes it more fun. I sip on a hot cup of herbal tea, play Chopin, light a candle, and enjoy some snacks—all while I am grading. Before I know it, I'm done. Nothing replaces work.

The coolest thing about becoming wealthy is generosity! Don't forget to share! This will bring you more joy than accumulating stuff.

Spend more on memories and less on things. Picnic in the park. Travel with your loved ones. Create special moments of celebration.

The Fray

You can stay below the fray, enter the fray, or rise above the fray. When you are below, you choose to stay ignorant of the fray. It is not something that interests you. When you enter the fray, you enter the drama. It is something you want to fight for, something you believe in, and a cause that strikes a chord within you. When you stay above the fray, you choose peace rather than the battle of the fray. It is a cause you understand, but you are also able to see it from a different perspective than others.

Choose your battles wisely, for they define you. Be selective when deciding to stay below, within, or when rising above the fray.

Soil

Luscious, mystical, rich, black soil; moist and full of nutrients, thick with potential, the womb of everything. Waiting to nurture a seed so that it might become a sunflower, a grapefruit tree, a climbing vine. Harboring ants and rabbits. Turning into mud, for baths and ancient bricks.

We dance on you, dig you, and build upon you. We bury our dead in your depths. We become you when gravity and time calls, then our spirits fly.

Dear soil, you are a life-infused manifested blessing from the realm of Original Imagination.

Your Storybook

How will your storybook read? What will you write? Your life is your story. What chapters are already written? What chapters are yet to be decided? You can choose many storylines, so decide today your next narrative.

Ink
(a song about writing)

Verse I:
I'm feeling creative, gonna get my pen and paper
I'm talkin' bout' my favorite pen with the tiny black tip
It fills the wood grain and it won't drip.

My words never run together. They just lay on the page like
fuzz on a feather.

The sentences are happy to be forming a thought
The question mark is asking just to have a dot.
The q's like to curl and the o's like to whirl
Around and around but they never fall down.

Chorus:
I'm happy listening to the sound of ink sinking into paper
Happy listening to the sound of thoughts going deeper
Happy listening to the sound of ink sinking into paper
Happy listening to the sound of ink sink

Verse II:
Each time that I lay my pen down to go to the sink or stop to think, this slice of tree I see before me is like a lady in waiting for her next ink drink.

My words never run together; they just lay on the page like fuzz on a feather.

The dangling participles hang around, waiting on a verb or a proper noun.
The comma interrupts. The T hits a peak
Every letter unique as the page starts to speak.

43

Different

Step outside of labels that you or others may have placed on you. If someone tells you that you are different, take it as a compliment. Celebrate the unique aspects that make you, *you.* Your difference gives you specific skills and capabilities to accomplish your life's mission. Find your passion, protect it, and use your special gifts to make a difference. You are different. Embrace your difference.

A short, funny memory:

My dad, who was a pastor, liked to tell a story about a preacher who was speaking in a church about the differences between men and women. The preacher said, "There's only a little bit of difference between a man and a woman." A drunk man in the back of the church stood up and, slurring his words, said, "Thank God for that *little bit* of difference!"

Amen.

44

Lessons

Are we using our past as a stumbling block or a springboard?
Lesson learned. Springboard higher!

45

Sacred Space

Create a space somewhere that is exclusively your space. A sacred space where the only thing you do in that space is take time for you—a place to pray, meditate, write, play music, paint, scrapbook, knit, whatever you do to create. Make sure the space does not require a lot of work when you enter; make it simple and peaceful. In many Eastern religions, believers have a room in their home that is dedicated to prayer/meditation and their holy book.

In order to purify and clear the air in your environment, change it up by removing objects (pictures, jewelry, furniture, dried flowers, etc.) that represent a time when you felt broken.

Instead, fill your sacred space with minimal items of beauty, or with nothing, and let your spirit and God's presence mingle to create a divine and holy atmosphere.

Bliss

What are you doing when you are the happiest, when you are blissful? What makes you want to get up in the morning and whistle or hum or sing? What is it? How do you take that feeling and extend it to last throughout your day? If money was of no concern, what would you do with your life? This one precious time that you get to be on this planet as you is special. You, with your skin color, bright eyes, and interesting hairstyle are bliss personified. What brings you bliss? Lean into it, dive into it, swim under the waters of bliss, and live! By living in your bliss, you will inspire others to live in theirs. Are you feeling blissful? Think on bliss. Selah.

47

Our Best

If we do our best, we can't blame ourselves for things that don't work out the way we think they should have. When making major decisions for our life, it is important to study, seek wise counsel, and trust our instincts. Make the decision and don't look back. When working on a project, it is important to do our very best, go the extra mile, and then release it. Our best can look different depending on our season of life.

Your best is good enough.

48

Change

We are never "stuck." As the saying goes, "The only thing constant is change." We must surrender to change. If you take the first steps, the Universe will align with you and help you accomplish your wishes. When you move, God moves. When you knock, doors open. What you seek, you find. Our steps are ordered for goodness.

If you don't like the state of things, don't worry, change will happen.

Even change, changes.

This is a law of the Universe.

49

Words

Let your words be positive, encouraging, full of goodness and wisdom. And with this practice, you will be a powerful force in the world. If God created the Universe with words or with a song, you, too, can create your world with your own words. Speak life, and your life will manifest.

Positivity

We have a superpower. It is our own thoughts. What thoughts are you thinking? What are you telling yourself? I heard a guy the other day keep telling himself how stupid he was and what an idiot he was. I knew that he was neither stupid nor an idiot, but he kept reaffirming this to himself. Eventually, you will believe what you tell yourself. My mom was putting herself down one day, and my dad said, "No one talks bad about my wife, not even my wife." Every time those thoughts come, replace them with exactly the opposite. Replace "I am so stupid" with "I am brilliant." Replace "I am ugly" with "I am a foxy, gorgeous dame."

Positive thinking is a superpower we can acquire with practice.

Create

You might think you're not creative, but I promise you there is a creative side of you that is dying to express itself. Take time to be creative—not perfect, creative. Creativity is a purifying and refreshing river that can flow through you and wash away cobwebs of sadness, disappointment, and insecurity to carve new pathways.

You are a creative being. Create and renew.

Passion Energizes

When we are passionate, we have boundless energy. When we are confused, we suffer mental and physical exhaustion. Take time to find your passion. Stop and think about what moves you from bliss to action. Something you enjoy that is relaxing might not light a fire within you. But when you are passionate, it is hard to stop yourself from taking action.

It is said that the Orthodox Christian monks on Mount Athos need little sleep because their prayer life energizes them. The monks have found a passion for spiritual warfare through prayer in the arena on the mountain.

What stirs passion within you?

53

Be Selective

Be selective with whom you share your dreams. Some people are not worthy of knowing them. Your dreams are like pearls, precious and hidden within your heart until you choose to reveal them. Scripture says, "Don't throw your pearls before swine, lest they trample them, then turn and attack you." Your dreams are sacred.

Be selective of who receives the privilege of hearing your hopes and dreams.

Good Morning

This is a morning song that I have been singing to my daughter since she was a baby. She now sings it with me.

> *Good Morning to the Morning!*
> *Good Morning to the Morning!*
> *Good Morning to the Morning!*
> *Good Morning! Good Morning!*

> *Good Morning to the birds and the bees,*
> *the flowers and the trees,*
> *To you and me,*
> *Good Morning! Good Morning!*

What a joy to greet the morning sun, the light of creation. What a joy to join the creatures and plants that are also waking and singing good morning to the morning!

Good Morning!

55

You Are Beautiful

Just a short reminder, "You are Beautiful!"

You are.

Release to Embrace

If we hold onto something too tight, we can smother it, but when we open our grip, it can breathe and we can embrace it.

Sometimes we hold on tight to things out of fear. We are afraid to make any changes because it might knock down the whole house of cards. We are afraid to change our structure, our routine, for fear that our life might collapse around us. We are afraid we might lose what we are holding. We like to be in control of our lives—and sometimes the lives of others too.

If we don't learn to release, we cannot embrace.

Surrender the pen of your life to God, the Magnificent Author, who loves you beyond your imagination.

God

How do you define God?

For me, God is . . .

The essence that gives matter meaning.

The force that laws obey.

The mystery that knows all things.

The incessant renewal in our cells and every living thing.

The clock that determines spring, summer, autumn, and winter.

The wisdom that tells baby birds when to hatch, and human and animal babies when to emerge from wombs.

God is not just a lonely energy field out in space, separate from us.

If this renewal force of Life did not exist, neither would we.

We are the proof that God exists.

God is Love, Lover, and Beloved, a Triune dance that is complete in One. We are invited to join this dance of Love, to let Love flow out of this dance and pour onto others. This is God, the Creator of the Universe, the Everlasting.

God.

58

Trust

One of the greatest lessons we can learn in life is to trust in God.

Trust that God wants the best for us.

Trust that God loves us.

Trust that life and death are in the hands of God.

True trust brings us peace.

365 Gifts

One day, when I was feeling low, I asked God to give me a reason to live each day. My mind began to flood with all of the lovely gifts of life. I wrote down 365 gifts, one for each day of the year. Oh, what wondrous gifts are HERE on Earth:

1. The sensation of snow melting on your tongue

2. Growing an herb garden

3. A sweet violin solo

4. A baby's laugh

5. Touching velvet

6. Holding hands for the first time with someone you admire

7. The sparkles in sand

8. Déjà vu

9.   Waking up after a good dream

10. Wind blowing across your face

11. A budding cactus

12. Colors

13. Music

14. Sliding into clean sheets after a day of hard work

15. Brightly shining stars on a dark night

16. The animals of the ocean

17. A good, hard sneeze

18. Warm sun on your back

19. A hot bubble bath with candles

20. Fire

21. The gurgling sound of a brook in the woods

22. The rustling of the leaves as they dance in the wind

23. A stormy day with a good book and hot tea

24. Laughing till your stomach hurts

25. The smell of morning after a night of rain

26. Fluffy house slippers

27. Chocolate

28. The feel of fuzz on peaches

29. Planting a seed and watching it grow

30. Inventing something useful

31. Kittens

32. A perfectly ripe banana

33. A dancer who seems suspended in midair

34. A child's imagination

35. Miracles

36. Unexpected discoveries

37. Rewards for hard work

38. A mother's love

39. The taste of honeysuckle

40. Touching a frog's back with your bare hands

41. Trying a new recipe

42. The most delicious meal you've ever had

43. The day you passed your driving test

44. A happy ending to a movie

45. Home-canned dill pickles

46. A competitive game

47. An ice cold drink at a sporting event.

48. Golfing your best game

49. Watching a baby enter the world

50. A surprise

51. Running through a sprinkler on a hot, humid day

52. The first day you can breathe through your nose after a long cold

53. Wearing your favorite scent

54. Rescuing a puppy from the pound

55. Licorice

56. Waking up in the morning and feeling joy

57. A warm hug

58. A best friend

59. Finding something you thought you had lost forever

60. Cinnamon sticks in hot cider

61. The red, gold, and orange leaves of fall

62. Roasting marshmallows over a bonfire

63. Homemade rolls

64. Making snow angels

65. Sushi

66. Crossing a border

67. Digging your feet in warm sand

68. Anticipation

69. Satisfaction

70. Raising your arms and yelling your name as loud as you can

71. Winning at dominoes

72. A watermelon-scented candle

73. Listening to a Blues record that moves your soul

74. Dancing with no inhibitions

75. Reaping the good harvest you've sown

76.   Looking into the big eyes of a cow

77.   Being followed by a baby lamb

78.   Blinding sparkling snow

79.   Icicles

80.   Flying down the hill of a roller coaster

81.   Dreaming great dreams for your future

82.   Licking chocolate-chip cookie batter off the beaters

83.   A smile

84.   Stretching exercises

85. A home remedy that heals

86. Whipped cream and strawberries

87. Completing a project

88. Giving a gift for which someone has asked

89. Pretending you're the ruler of the Universe

90. Herbs, oils, and aromatherapy

91. Believing

92. Splurging on some new clothes

93. Southern cookin'

94. Seeing a dolphin jump out of the ocean

95. Nursing an injured animal back to health

96. Money in your pocket and a big outdoor flea market

97. Bowling a strike

98. Grasping the wheel of your new car

99. Making a choice

100. Celebrating your day of birth

101. Riding bareback on a running horse

102. A picnic on a hill with all of your favorite food

103. Learning to play an instrument

104. Singing in a choir

105. Sleeping in a feather bed

106. A dream that comes true

107. Walking in a field of wildflowers

108. Learning to sail

109. Flying across a lake in a speed boat

110. Swimming underwater with colorful fish

111. Stoking logs in a fireplace

112. Hot, sugar-topped biscuits baked in a black iron skillet

113. Sitting under a weeping willow tree next to a stream

114. Learning to fly

115. Adopting a child

116. Writing a poem

117. Picking out supplies from an art store

118. Realizing that there is no one who loves, thinks, looks, laughs, creates like you

119. Marrying the man/woman of your dreams

120. Calling your children for dinner

121. Cuddling your baby for the first time

122. Remembering a debt owed to a friend and paying it

123. Giving anything to a homeless brother or sister

124. The art of listening

125. Crying with a friend over his/her loss

126. Skiing and then soaking in a hot tub

127. Learning a magic trick

128. Digging up vegetables from your own garden

129. Spicy chili

130. The call of a long-lost friend

131. Trusting completely

132. Thanking your parents for caring for you

133. Questioning a new rule

134. A pink-and-orange sunset

135. Dawn breaking across the ocean

136. Making room for someone new at your dinner table

137. Watching an artist sculpt

138. Wind whipping your hair

139. The smell of a hot cherry pie

140. Divine interventions

141. Rocking the boat

142. A family reunion

143. The ringing of a bell in a clock tower

144. Touring a castle

145. Kissing your grandma's cheek

146. Repeating a story your grandfather told you

147. Fixing a broken toy

148. Filling your calendar with things you enjoy

149. Rewarding yourself with a manicure and pedicure

150. Love butterflies in your belly

151. The twinkle in a lover's eye

152. Bringing a hot meal to someone who can't leave home

153. A long, deep sigh of relief

154. Watching a baby taste new flavors

155. Receiving the benefit of an investment

156. A rocking chair

157. Receiving a diploma

158. Picking out a card that makes you laugh out loud

159. Swinging on a porch swing

160. Hearing your father say, "I'm proud of you."

161. Noticing a deer watching you

162. An art museum

163. Dressing up and going to a play or opera

164. Drawing on the sidewalk with sand rocks

165. Riding the wildest looking horse on a carousel

166. Watching a butterfly stretch her wings as she emerges from her chrysalis

167. The coo of a dove

168. A pat on the back

169. The trusting look in a puppy's eyes

170. The smell of sweet, mowed grass

171. Participating in a ritual

172. Flying down a hill on a red bicycle

173. Standing under a waterfall

174. Black-and-white photography

175. Performance art

176. Feeling productive

177. A pimento-cheese sandwich

178. Listening to a recording of your own voice

179. Riding a Harley Davidson motorcycle

180. The feeling of empty relief after a hard cry

181. S'mores

182. The vibrato of an old soul singer

183. A koi pond

184. Sweet tea

185. Homemade pear jelly

186. The scent of Egyptian Goddess incense

187. Buying something from a child's lemonade stand

188. The bloom of a flower

189. Complete silence

190. A philosophical chat with a philosophical friend

191. Lightning bugs

192. Buying your first home

193. Popcorn and a great flick

194. Holding hands in a movie theater

195. A bride in a white gown, veil, and train

196. A racing black-steel locomotive

197. Chocolate cake made from scratch with chocolate fudge icing

198. Blueberry cheesecake

199. Double-dip ice cream in a sugar cone

200. The smell of pine trees

201. Licking cookie dough off the beaters

202. Happening upon a sawdust tent revival

203. Preparing a candlelight dinner

204. Wishes that come true

205. Peacocks

206. The howl of a wolf

207. Flying a kite

208. Solving a mystery

209. Climbing a tree

210. Developing pictures in a darkroom

211. Imagining what is beyond the horizon

212. Playing a tambourine

213. Visiting a planetarium

214. The promise in a rainbow

215. Thunder and lightning

216. The story of the ugly duckling

217. Wishing on a falling star

218. The unpredictable hues of a sunset

219. A clear mountain stream

220. Sugar cubes

221. Coloring easter eggs

222. Making a pumpkin jack-o-lantern

223. The smell of a petunia

224. Finding the constellations in the sky

225. Jumping in piles of fall leaves

226. Wearing something outrageous

227. Chewing pink gum and blowing bubbles

228. Your childhood home

229. Saving a human life

230. Receiving an unexpected letter

231. Rekindling an old flame

232. Tracing your ancestry

233. Laughing till you ache inside

234. Prisms of light

235. Looking at a caricature drawing of yourself

236. A dynamite rock collection

237. Discovering a hobby that becomes your favorite

238. Dew on the petal of a lily

239. Burying your feet in warm sand

240. Learning to whistle

241. Painting your toenails bright pink

242. Discovering your shadow

243. A spontaneous road trip

244. Talking till dawn with a new friend

245. Waking up and feeling joy

246. A child's laughter

247. Arms that reach for you

248. Wearing large mirrored sunglasses

249. Hot Krispy Kreme doughnuts

250. A cedar sauna

251. Communicating in a new language

252. Discovering a new color

253. A bargain

254. Being lost in an intriguing novel

255. Walking through low, misty clouds

256. Tortilla chips and spicy salsa

257. A blank sheet of paper and a head full of ideas

258. Drums

259. Fresh-squeezed lemonade in a cold, sugar-rimmed glass

260. Free tickets to the Superbowl

261. Questioning and not needing the answers

262. A craving that is fulfilled

263. Reaching a peak

264. Fireworks

265. Watching a newborn colt frolic across a field

266. A guiltless thrill

267. A caramel apple

268. Cotton candy

269. A lesson from Winnie the Poo

270. Ice skating on a pond

271. A perfect mixture

272. Unconditional love

273. Pure delight

274. Ecstasy

275. Receiving an answer from a sacred text

276. Watching a chick hatch

277. Tobogganing down a snowy, steep hill with a load of friends

278. Getting a gold tooth

279. A first kiss

280. A Sunday afternoon nap

281. Sucking on a lollipop

282. Gospel rhythms

283. Trying to hold in a laugh during a quiet ceremony

284. Breaking a bad habit

285. Starting a good habit

286. Getting a new hairdo

287. Marching to a chant

288. River rocks

289. Discovering that the phrase "there are no absolute truths" is trying to be an absolute truth

290. Never saying never

291. Double Dutch jump roping

292. Barrel racing at a rodeo

293. Crossing off projects on a "things to do" list

294. Being a mystery to everyone at a costume ball

295. The hope of life after death

296. Dancing till you drop

297. Red clay cliffs

298. Exploring a cave

299. Restoring an old house

300. Speeding in a loud hot rod

301. Winning

302. Tie-dyeing

303. Looking through a telescope and seeing the craters on the moon

304. Lingering inside a beautiful moment

305. An electric blanket on a freezing night

306. Wearing colors that clash, for shock value

307. Skinny-dipping

308. Blowing dandelion fuzz

309. Playing marbles

310. The art of low-rider cars

311. Cookouts

312. Nursing a plant back to life

313. Discovering a common interest with an old friend

314. Popsicles with ice cream in the middle

315. Tapping into a different realm

316. Reading your old diaries

317. Exotic fish

318. Wearing an oversized flannel shirt

319. The parables of Jesus Christ

320. Daydreaming

321. Animation

322. Honoring an elder

323. Making a new tradition

324. The warmth of a soft blanket

325. Oil painting

326. Studying a culture other than your own

327. Sculpting clay on a potter's wheel

328. Sneaking behind the curtain at a circus

329. Learning to shoot a bow and arrow

330. Wearing flowers in your hair

331. Riding a running horse bareback thru green fields

332. Purchasing a unique piece of art for your home

333. Gaining a new perspective

334. The glint of light on the ripples of water

335. Tastebuds

336. Freedom from evil control

337. Singing off-key in an elevator full of people

338. Decorating your new home

339. Forgiveness

340. Proving that you were falsely accused

341. Words that rhyme

342. Our solar system

343. Undiscovered lands

344. Fossils

345. Clues

346. Surviving a near-fatal disease

347. Being given a second chance

348. Chunky yarn

349. Seeing cloud pictures in the sky

350. A hot-stone massage

351. The song "Purple Rain"

352. Receiving recognition for your creativity

353. Clapping off beat

354. Matching socks

355. Confronting a fear

356. Learning to swim

357. Surfing a wave

358. Exploring a rain forest

359. Experiencing a new texture

360. Pulling out a splinter from someone's finger

361. Anything considered eclectic

362. Speaking words that seem to come from somewhere beyond you

363. Realizing that without struggles there are no victories

364. A deep, ancient knowing that you are not alone

365. You

366. And one to grow on—God

367. Add yours

....

....

....

....

....

60

The Secret Code

There is a secret code hidden in chapter 59 of this book. It is a great mystery.

Clue: Once you understand this mystery, your journey of life will shift. It will set you free in ways you have never imagined. Your world will come alive. Colors will appear more vibrant. You will see people from a new perspective. You may even find a new interest in the cosmos.

The code

10R	73A
12B	76C
21F-1	91F
23A	96D
33G	366Q
53B	

About the Author

Dr. Sharenda Roam is a professor of Religious Studies.

She lives with her husband, daughter, and pups.

She finds joy in mossy forests, sacred books, art, candles, soulful music, tea, and laughter with her loved ones.

Beloved

www.ingramcontent.com/pod-product-compliance
Lightning Source LLC
Chambersburg PA
CBHW061745020426
42331CB00006B/1364